Grieving SUICIDE

A 30-DAY DEVOTIONAL
FOR HEALING
AFTER LOSS AND GRIEF

BY SUSAN STOTTS

Grieving Suicide: A 30-Day Devotional for Healing After Loss and Grief

Copyright © 2021 By Susan Stotts

ISBN: 9798517046697

Cover Design by: Tehsin Gull

Printed in the United States of America. All rights reserved under International Copyright Law. Contents and/or cover may not be reproduced in whole or in part in any form without the express written consent of the author.

All Scripture quotations are from The Passion Translation® unless otherwise notated. Copyright © 2017, 2018 by Passion & Fire Ministries, Inc. Used by permission. All rights reserved. ThePassionTranslation.com.

Scripture quotations marked (NIV) are taken from the Holy Bible, New International Version®, NIV®. Copyright © 1973, 1978, 1984, 2011 by Biblica, Inc.™ Used by permission of Zondervan. All rights reserved worldwide. www.zondervan.com The "NIV" and "New International Version" are trademarks registered in the United States Patent and Trademark Office by Biblica, Inc.™

Scripture quotations marked (NKJV) are taken from the New King James Version®. Copyright © 1982 by Thomas Nelson. Used by permission. All rights reserved.

Disclaimer: Although the author has made every effort to ensure that the information in this book was correct at press time and while this publication is designed to provide accurate information regarding the subject matter covered, the author assumes no responsibility for errors, inaccuracies, omissions, or any other inconsistencies. The author herein and hereby disclaims any liability to any party for any loss, damage, or disruption caused by errors or omissions, whether such errors or omissions result from negligence, accident, or any other cause. This publication is meant as a source of valuable information, comfort, and encouragement for the reader; however, it is not meant as a substitute for direct expert assistance or to replace any necessary counseling. If such level of assistance is required, the services of a competent professional should be sought.

Dedication

I dedicate this devotional to Jesus Christ, my Lord. Because of your great faithfulness and because of the depths of your love, healing has come, and restoration has come. I owe you my all.

Contents

Foreword 9
Introduction 11
Stage 1. Denial **13**
Day 1 15
Day 2 19
Day 3 23
Day 4 27
Day 5 31
Day 6 35
Stage 2. Anger **39**
Day 7 41
Day 8 45
Day 9 49
Day 10 53
Day 11 57
Day 12 61
Stage 3. Bargaining & Regret **65**
Day 13 67
Day 14 71

Day 15 75
Day 16 79
Day 17 83
Day 18 87
Stage 4. Depression 91
Day 19 93
Day 20 97
Day 21 101
Day 22 105
Day 23 109
Day 24 113
Stage 5. Acceptance 117
Day 25 119
Day 26 123
Day 27 127
Day 28 131
Day 29 135
Day 30 139
Conclusion 143
I Pray You Were Blessed 145
Acknowledgments 147
About the Author 149

Foreword

From the moment Susan first told me her life story, I knew God had prepared her to carry a message of hope for those of us who have been left to gather the shattered pieces that suicide leaves behind.

Susan's life has been scarred by multiple suicides, but she has allowed God to do a work of healing in her life – the same healing she shares on the pages of this book.

There were nearly 50,000 deaths by suicide in America last year. Sadly, there are many nations around the world who have even more devastating statistics. This is a global epidemic.

My family has also survived the devastation of a life cut short without warning. That's why I'm personally grateful for this brave and important book.

We all heal at our own pace. Your journey is your own. These thirty devotions are just a beginning, but I pray they will move you forward as you seek to discover healing after loss and grief.

Donna Partow

Bestselling Author, *This Isn't the Life I Signed Up For, But I'm Finding Hope & Healing*

Introduction

Truth be told, *Grieving Suicide: A 30-Day Devotional for Healing After Loss and Grief* was not something I was looking to write. Nevertheless, the more I researched loss and grief, the more I realized how many people are experiencing this undeniable and unavoidable pain.

Grief has a way of making us feel exposed and vulnerable. It is sometimes difficult to discern if other people are acting in sympathy or pity. The pain of loss cannot be equated to tripping, falling, and getting up again. Many people who have not experienced tremendous loss have little compassion. They often expect you to just *get over it*. They do not understand that there is a process that cannot be put on a schedule.

This devotional will help you take the journey with God's help, from grieving to healing. You can't fix this. It's not healthy to stuff your emotions into a "Do Not Access" file in your heart. You have to choose to feel your feelings—whatever they may be.

I know grief. I understand loss. We have become reluctant travel companions. My younger brother took the life of another human being and then took his own life. Six years later, my older brother OD'd on his 50th birthday. It was two weeks before anyone found him. The funeral home removed the body. My two younger brothers had to clean up the bedroom where he was found, and my older sister and I cleaned out his apartment.

This is just part of my story. Numerous others have tried to end their lives, and I have helped them through this process.

I consider myself a strong person. I believed I could walk through this tunnel of darkness on my own. I was wrong. It's one of the biggest mistakes people make. It's hard to say the word suicide, let alone admit that someone you love took his or her own life. People who want to empathize don't know what to say; they get uncomfortable and act weird. While their heart's intent may be to help, it only makes us feel worse.

In recent years, a growing number of people have wanted to give up on life. They have no hope, no desire to live. They may not have a relationship with the Lord or feel that their pain and hopelessness are bigger than God. This is one of the enemy's greatest lies. The truth is that God loves them just as He loves you and me. He has not forsaken us.

This book will help you:

- ❖ Understand the emotions you are feeling
- ❖ Feel God's comfort and compassion while mourning
- ❖ Recognize that you are not alone
- ❖ Walkthrough the stages of grief and loss
- ❖ Learn creative ways to keep the memories of your loved one alive
- ❖ Move forward in the healing process

I urge you to be proactive in the quiet reflections at the end of each day. I want you to receive the benefits from what God taught me and apply them to your life. You are loved, and you are not alone. The tears will dry, and comfort will come. But for now, just breathe.

Many Blessings,

Susan

STAGE 1

Denial

Day 1

Yet when holy lovers of God cry out to him with all their hearts, the Lord will hear them and come to rescue them from all their troubles. The Lord is close to all whose hearts are crushed by pain.
—Psalm 34:17-18a (TPT)

Has time ever seemed to stand still for you? It happens most often in moments of extreme joy, pain, or trauma. When I received the news that my brother had taken the life of someone and then took his life, the world seemed to stop spinning. Everything was moving around me, but my world stopped as the arrow of what I heard pierced my heart.

Maybe you felt that way, too—when words cannot even describe the devastation. Your entire being has just entered a state of shock. As you begin to comprehend the reality of the news, the arrow settles into your soul.

You are not alone.

The Lord is close to those who are crushed by pain, whose hearts are bleeding from the arrow of the inexplicable. We try to deny what has happened. We don't want to believe that it is true. We try to reason away the pain of the circumstances, but logic isn't helpful in these times.

You are not alone. God is with you. He is still Emmanuel—God with us.

It's okay to cry. It's okay to feel numb. It's okay not to know how or what to feel. But I'd encourage you to allow Jesus to comfort you. He longs to fill your soul with His love, His hope, and His peace. He wants to bring you strength.

PRAYER

Holy God, help me. My heart is hurting. There is so much I don't understand. Right now, I don't even know if I'm going to be okay. Your Word says that when I cry out to You, You are near and will rescue me. Rescue me, Lord. I don't even know what that looks like. Open my heart and eyes to see that You are doing what you promised me. I need You. My family needs You. Heal the hearts of all those affected by this tragedy. In Jesus' name. Amen

QUIET PONDERINGS

Take a few moments and get quiet. You may or may not want to play some soft worship or instrumental music. Sit down. Be still, and just breathe. Allow God to breathe His breath upon you. Ask God to quiet your soul with His love and fill you with His peace. If you have a Scripture verse that brings you peace, you may want to read it over repeatedly and allow its truth to bring you comfort.

DAY 1

Write Out Your Own Prayer:

Day 2

His massive arms are wrapped around you, protecting you. You can run under his covering of majesty and hide. His arms of faithfulness are a shield keeping you from harm.
—Psalm 91:4 (TPT)

God is with you. Can you picture His arms of love wrapped around you? Can you imagine running to Him to find a place of shelter, a place to hide from the rest of the world?

When our hearts and minds are hurting, we want somewhere to hide. We want to get away from the everyday tasks of life and hide. God wants to be our hiding place. He wants to shelter us from harm.

God knows what we need. He walks with us on this journey of grief as we struggle to find a new normal. Envision the arms of God holding you, and allow your body, soul, and spirit to rest in His protection. His arms are like a shield hovering over us, protecting us as we yield to His love.

What does a shield do? It provides protection from our enemies. What does it look like? What is it made of? What if God's faithfulness was like an invisible forcefield that covered us completely? What if the strength of this forcefield depended on our belief in its reality? What if the more we believed that God was faithful in every circumstance, the stronger and more impenetrable His shield and forcefield around us became? Choose to believe that God is faithful—even when it hurts.

Know this: God is fighting for you. He is not against you. Choose to receive His rest even in the midst of this battle.

PRAYER

Holy God, my mind is spinning. I have so many questions without answers. I'm in disbelief that this is now a part of my story, a part of my family's story. I need You. Help me to feel Your massive arms wrapped around me, protecting me. I run under the covering of Your majesty and hide. I believe that Your arms of faithfulness are a shield and will keep me from harm. Be my hiding place today. In Jesus' name. Amen.

QUIET PONDERINGS

Quiet yourself before the Lord. Put some soft worship music on and ponder what you just read. Dialogue with God about His shield. Thank Him in faith for that shield. Wait on Him. He will answer. Take a few moments and journal what God speaks to your heart.

DAY 2

Write Out Your Own Prayer:

Day 3

*I am truly his rose, the very theme of his song.
I'm overshadowed by his love,
like a lily growing in the valley!*
—Song of Songs: 2:1

Do you remember the first time you received flowers— *maybe even roses?*

Was it a special day? Did a particular person give them to you? How did you feel after you received the exquisite flowers? Do you remember the fragrance, the aroma, the place you were when you received them?

Roses are often associated with love and romance. There are many different colors and kinds of roses; each one has a different meaning. Even the number of roses received can have a distinct meaning. I love the Song of Songs and how God calls it "His Divine Romance."

God said that we are the "theme of his song" (Song 2:1). This is a personal and intimate thing to say. Why would God say this to us? Because He overshadows and covers us with His love. Powerful words!

Ponder this: God desires to connect our hearts with His. He is passionate about us. He wants to fill every empty place within us with His unquenchable love.

Our emotions often overtake us as we try to fathom why a loved one took his or her own life. Our emotions are riding on a rollercoaster that they never wanted to ride. What if we asked God to be our passenger on this ride? What if we allowed our soul to receive some of His love to fill that place of unpredictability?

Our God relentlessly pursues our affections. He is faithful. He has proven Himself continuously through His words, deeds, and actions. God is always speaking. However, sometimes things in this world, like the news or our emotions, muffle His voice.

As we take time to allow God to cover us with His love, we learn to rest in Him. We will grow in confidence and become stronger. We'll get to a place where we find that we can breathe again, maybe even hope again. But for right now, it's okay to cry. Let God's love cover you like a blanket and just rest.

PRAYER

Thank you, Lord, for pursuing me with Your passionate love. I am so grateful for Your love during heartache and pain. Let Your LOVE become LOUDER than the pain and loss. Help me to love You in return. In Jesus' name. Amen.

QUIET PONDERINGS

Quiet yourself before the Lord. Put some soft worship music on and ponder that you are God's long-stemmed rose. You are the theme of His song. Ask the Lord to help You hear the song that He is singing over you.

DAY 3

Write Out Your Own Prayer:

Day 4

*For he has not despised my cries of deep despair.
He's my first responder to my sufferings, and when I was in pain, he
was there all the time and heard the cries of the afflicted.*
—Psalm 22:24

Most likely, you understand what it's like to cry from the depths of your soul. You know it carries with it a sound that is difficult to describe.

When my brother took the life of another human and then his own, I was an immature Christian. The pain, coupled with questions, was more than I could bear. How could my brother be a judge and jury all at once? How could he make such a decision and carry it through? My brother must have been so full of pain.

Psalm 22:24 says it all. As I cried in deep despair, God was my first responder. He didn't look the other way when I was in pain. God is with you. He is not deterred by our pain, our conflict, or even our questions. He sits with us in our mourning, desiring to comfort us, not condemn us.

Honestly, it took me ten years to forgive my brother for the pain he caused others. Nevertheless, God heard my cries of deep despair. He didn't turn away from my pain. In fact, He helped me face my pain which in turn brought true healing.

I am forever grateful. God is not a respecter of persons. He will do the same for you.

How does God help us in our suffering? He sent people to love on me, to grieve with me, and to listen to me. People who listened without judgment. People who displayed the love of God. I pray that God will send people like that into your life; take a moment right now to ask Him to.

PRAYER

Father, thank you that You're not afraid of my pain or despair. Nothing is too big or too messy for You. I appreciate that about You. Thank you for hearing my cries of deep despair and for being my first responder in my time of need. Thank you for continuing to heal my heart. Please send people into my life who will love me, grieve with me and listen to me without judgment. In Jesus' name. Amen.

QUIET PONDERINGS

Quiet yourself before the Lord. Put some soft worship music on and just rest in God's presence. You may want to share what's on your mind and heart with God. It's okay. He's not afraid of your emotions or thoughts.

DAY 4

Write Out Your Own Prayer:

Day 5

Yahweh is my best friend and my shepherd. I always have more than enough. He offers a resting place for me in his luxurious love. His tracks take me to an oasis of peace near the quiet brook of bliss. That's where he restores and revives my life. He opens before me the right path and leads me along in his footsteps of righteousness so that I can bring honor to his name.
—Psalm 23:1-3

Have you ever read something that is supposed to bring you comfort, but it doesn't? Some days our hearts reject the truth. When this happens, it's important to acknowledge and even validate your current state. We can't force ourselves to feel something we don't.

What we can do is give ourselves grace and mercy. We can acknowledge that the Lord is our Shepherd. We can choose to believe that He desires to restore our souls—even when we don't feel restored or revived just yet.

However, when our world has been turned upside down and inside out, it's a little harder to receive these beautiful truths. Receiving can be especially difficult in times of grief. It's okay. Give yourself space to breathe and receive what your heart will allow.

As time passes, you'll find it easier to run to the Lord. God's LOVE is really like no other. He is true to His Word.

Life as you know it has changed. Currently, the waters are muddy and murky as we think about the ones we have lost. Our loved one's choice is causing us deep-seated pain. But what about our loved one's pain? What feelings caused him or her to believe that death was the only answer?

What if we silenced the voices of inquisition and accusation in our minds for a moment? What if we chose to lay down in the green pastures of God's comfort? What if we decided to drink from God's pure fountain? What if we asked God to restore and revive our aching soul? What if we offered Him our confusion and the broken pieces of our soul?

What if God was truly able to bring us to an oasis where we learned to rest? God can create the space we need to enable us to breathe again, hope again, and live again.

PRAYER

Father, thank you that You long to restore and revive my soul. Thank you for offering me a resting place in Your luxurious love. I say yes! Yes, I accept Your resting place. Yes, I accept the oasis of peace near a quiet brook of bliss. Help me to quiet the voices in my heart and mind. Quiet my soul with Your love. In Jesus' name. Amen.

QUIET PONDERINGS

Quiet yourself before the Lord. Put some soft worship music on and just rest in God's presence. Receive God's truth that He will restore and revive your soul. Let this truth bring comfort and peace deep into your heart. You may want to journal what you feel God is speaking.

DAY 5

Write Out Your Own Prayer:

Day 6

Even when your path takes me through the valley of deepest darkness, fear will never conquer me, for you already have! Your authority is my strength and my peace. The comfort of your love takes away my fear. I'll never be lonely, for you are near.
—Psalm 23:4

Grief often strikes without warning. A song, a word, a movie clip, and a sound can easily trigger feelings of loss or fear.

Not long after the murder and my brother's suicide, I remember that unexpected situations would jump up out of nowhere at me. For example, I attended a fourth of July parade in my small town. The Legion officers always start the parade with their rifles over their shoulders, marching. Suddenly, someone gave an order for the officers to stop.

BOOM! BOOM!

The officers shot blanks into the air. The next thing I knew, I took off running, trying to get away as fast as I could. Tears were streaming down my face, and I found it hard to breathe as I tried to get away from the crowd.

I knew the Legion officers were going to shoot their rifles; they did that every year. But because there was a gun involved in the murder and suicide, I unknowingly had new issues with guns.

My head knew that what the officers were doing was safe. I knew no one was going to get hurt; nevertheless, the sound triggered something deep inside of me. I asked God what happened to me. I asked Him why I reacted the way I did. He showed me that fear consumed me when I heard the shots fired.

When I heard the boom, my soul imagined how my brother's ex-girlfriend must have felt knowing that she couldn't get away. I'll admit that it took quite a bit of time to overcome the fear associated with guns. Nonetheless, fear will never conquer me because Jesus already has!

Jesus took my hand and walked me through the valley of deepest darkness and fear. He walked closely with me the whole way. He has never left my side, and He won't leave yours either.

God wants to walk you through the process of overcoming the trauma and triggers associated with the death of your loved one. He truly is an ever-present help in times of trouble.

PRAYER

Father, thank you for staying close to me through the deepest darkest valleys. Thank you that fear will never conquer me because you are with me. Your perfect love casts out fear. Your love is more powerful than fear. Thank you for healing my heart, Lord. In Jesus' name. Amen.

QUIET PONDERINGS

Quiet yourself before the Lord. Put some soft worship music on and just rest in God's presence. Allow His love to wash away your fears.

SELF CARE

You may want to ask a dear friend to go on a walk with you today. It will be helpful to get some fresh air. You may want to ask your friend if he or she will just listen to your heart and pray for you.

You may also want to get a massage. This will allow your body to release some tension and grief.

Write Out Your Own Prayer:

STAGE 2

Anger

Day 7

Are you weary, carrying a heavy burden? Come to me. I will refresh your life, for I am your oasis.
—Mathew 11:28

No one plans to live with grief. We don't wake up one morning and decide that we'll stand under a waterfall of sorrow. No, grief often hits us unexpectedly like an emotional freight train.

Grief acts differently in each one of us. For some, grief becomes almost like a rock; it's something solid to set our feet on when everything else seems to be like sinking sand. In this stage, our grief has turned to anger.

The quicker we embrace and release the anger, the quicker we will move through the process. If we attempt to suppress this emotion, it will only prolong the process.

I remember soon after my late husband graduated from this earth to his heavenly home, I went for a walk. I ended up in a gravel pit by my house. I was alone and screamed at God at the top of my lungs. I let God know all the reasons my husband needed to stay with me here on this earth:

- ❖ He was too young.
- ❖ His girls needed him.
- ❖ I needed him.

- What was I going to do without him?
- How do you become one by yourself when you work so hard to become one with two?

Yelling is not a part of my normal practice. Honestly, I really didn't feel any better for yelling. Nevertheless, I had questions deep inside my soul that needed to come out. If I had let these questions fester instead of confessing them to God, they could have turned into more profound issues.

Anger comes because there are so many unanswered questions. It may help to ask yourself the following questions:

1. Am I angry at the loved one who's gone? Why?
2. Am I angry at the situation? What about it makes me angry?
3. Am I angry at God? Why?

These are good questions to ask yourself. It can help you process through this crazy time in your life. Anger is a normal emotion in the process of grieving. Don't be afraid to confront it and work through it. Give yourself some time. It's not a once-and-done process.

PRAYER

Thank you, God, that anger doesn't surprise You. Thank you for seeing my pain through my outbursts. Thank you for being compassionate and loving. Come refresh me with Your presence. In Jesus' name. Amen.

QUIET PONDERINGS

Quiet yourself before the Lord. Put some soft worship music on and just rest in God's presence. You may want to ask yourself the questions from above or write out your own questions. If you need to find a place to yell or scream, do it. Allow yourself. If you don't want to scream, ask the Lord to help you find a positive outlet for your anger.

DAY 7

Write Out Your Own Prayer:

Day 8

But Lord, your nurturing love is tender and gentle. You are slow to get angry yet so swift to show your faithful love. You are full of abounding grace and truth.
—Psalm: 86:15

One of the most challenging things about suicide is that it steals your voice. It feels unjust because you didn't have an opportunity to talk about it with your loved one.

I was angry at my brothers because I didn't get to persuade them to live, to love. I didn't get to tell them how much pain their choice would cause me, my children, our family, and our friends.

I also didn't get to tell them how much I loved them.

Maybe they wanted those left behind to feel the pain of what they were feeling before the suicide. This was a question I had to ask myself.

As I struggled to find ways to work through my emotions, I discovered something practical that helped me even more than yelling. I found a quiet place and put some quiet worship music on, then I wrote a letter to my brothers. It was like I was talking to them. The Holy Spirit was with me, and I sensed His presence as I wrote. As I put pen to paper, everything just came out. The anger, the frustration, the pain, and the questions freely flowed from my soul into the letter.

This was an effective tool for me. I released a lot of pent-up emotions that day. I could finally put down my anger, and I didn't pick that anger up again. When the anger and other emotions would try to come back at me, I would simply read the letters to my brothers again.

As I shared via the letter with my deceased brothers the effect their choices had on me and my family, peace flooded my soul. I allowed God's nurturing love that is tender and gentle to guide my thoughts as I wrote whatever came to mind. God will meet us in whatever emotional state we are in. Emotions do not deter Him. Instead, God longs to reveal His truth to us so that we can release any negative emotions that are keeping us bound from receiving His love, joy, and peace.

PRAYER

Lord, thank you for Your love. Thank you so much for being so swift to show us that faithful love. We are so grateful for You. Thank you for being so gentle and kind when the emotions within us are so loud. In Jesus' name. Amen.

QUIET PONDERINGS

Quiet yourself before the Lord. Put some soft worship music on and just rest in God's presence. Write a letter to your loved one. Invite the Lord to sit with you. If you're having trouble starting the letter, ask Him to help you. Let it out. Don't hold back. Don't be afraid to be honest about what you're feeling and why you're feeling it. Don't be concerned about being proper. Ask what you need to ask. Say what you need to say.

Write a letter to your loved one who committed suicide. Release your negative emotions but also express your love for them.

DAY 8

Write Out Your Own Prayer:

Day 9

When I screamed out, "Lord, I'm doomed!" your fiery love was stirred, and you raced to my rescue. Whenever my busy thoughts were out of control, the soothing comfort of your presence calmed me down and overwhelmed me with delight.
—Psalm 94:18-19

God is so good to us!

God's presence brings comfort to our souls. He is not offended by the seemingly uncontrollable anger that attempts to overtake us in times of uncertainty. God gets it. He understands how our anger and life trauma can cause us to go from zero to a thousand in one moment. He knows how our minds spin off into a fury of unanswered whirlwinds. God's fiery love is stirred to rescue us at that moment. It may not feel like it or even look like it, but God doesn't lie.

As I was writing this book, my sister passed on to glory. I was told the doctors were keeping her comfortable because the pain was becoming unbearable for her. The doctors kept upping her pain meds. Though I believed for a different outcome, my sister passed less than a week later.

I was angry, and I could see that my husband was taking the brunt of my unspoken anger.

Lord, why am I taking this out on my husband?

The Lord showed me there were some things my husband and I needed to reconcile with each other. So, we sat down together and discussed the issues in an open, honest and healthy way.

Once my husband and I talked through some of our pain, I was able to see the underlying issues concerning my sister. I was able to understand the anger I had regarding her death.

I wouldn't have been able to move forward if it hadn't been for the soothing Word of the Lord. He comforted me. He showed me what I needed to do. He showed me the way forward. Know this: God is not a respecter of persons. He comforted me. He will comfort you. Ask Him to heal your heart. There is great comfort in His presence.

PRAYER

Thank you for Your comforting presence. Thank you that Your love is greater than our anger. Thank you for Your fiery love. Come now and overwhelm me in that fiery love. Overtake me now. In Jesus' name. Amen.

QUIET PONDERINGS

Quiet yourself before the Lord. Put some soft worship music on and just rest in God's presence. Ask Him if there are some unresolved issues in your heart. Ask Him if you are taking your anger out on others.

If there are issues, ask God to reveal how to resolve the anger. He'll give you an idea or a strategy. Remember, God only reveals to heal. You'll need to choose what to do with what He shows you. The sooner you act on His wisdom, the sooner your peace will be restored.

DAY 9

Write Out Your Own Prayer:

Day 10

So do not fear, for I am with you; do not be dismayed, for I am your God. I will strengthen you and help you; I will uphold you with my righteous right hand.
—Isaiah: 41:10 (NIV)

Have you ever been horrified by the intensity of your emotions?

I have. For me, it was a forbidden taboo to even look at anger, much less explore that it would be a necessary part of my healing process from my brothers' suicides.

I refused to acknowledge that I could ever be angry. My first response to anger was to run because of abusive people who struggled with anger in my past.

How did I deal with my suppressed anger? Clean. I was a cleaning machine. I could clean a house so fast it would make your head swim. I didn't want to talk, just clean. I would clean anything and everything to avoid facing the truth of my emotions. Cleaning was my way of releasing the adrenaline without yelling or screaming.

But then, I began to internalize the anger.

What did I need to do? What do you need to do? Sometimes, we must pause and take a look at *why* we are so angry. What is churning beneath the surface? What questions have gone unanswered? What pain has gone unattended?

Push past the fear of learning what angers you. Find out what it is. Explore why the anger is there. Anger is not merely a negative emotion. It is also an *indicator* that something needs attention. Anger is like an engine light in a car. When you see the light, you know the engine needs service.

It's okay to be angry. Anger often stems from injustice. The emotion is not bad to feel. It's what we do with the emotion that can cause trouble.

Unfortunately, that was not my experience with anger. What I knew about anger was that it was uncontrollable. It led to verbal and physical abuse. In my world, anger hurt people and left them feeling worthless.

So, I made a vow. I was not going to respond in anger. Sounds good, right? I wish it had been that easy.

I learned the hard way that there are effects from suppressing anger. Suppressing anger can result in serious health issues. Why? Our body holds pockets of trauma in our muscles, blood, organs, and even our brain. Anger leaves us in a place of turmoil, and it will fester until we deal with it.

God is so patient and loving with us. He will strengthen us and help us. He is our God, and we do not need to fear—even when it comes to our emotions.

I'll be the first to admit that it has taken me time and a lot of counseling to overcome the intimidation of the emotion of anger. Now, I'm able to look at anger through the eyes of the Lord--instead of through the eyes of trauma, fear, and pain.

Everyone walks through the stage of anger differently. Your process may look dramatically different than mine. Nevertheless, it is essential to deal with anger and allow God to restore your peace and joy.

PRAYER

Thank you, Lord, for not leaving me as You found me. Thank you for Your comforting presence. Thank you that You give me strength and uphold me in Your righteous right hand. I want to face my anger, but at the same time, I don't. Will You help me? Will You heal the pain that aches within my soul? I need Your strength right now. In Jesus' name. Amen.

QUIET PONDERINGS

Quiet yourself before the Lord. Put some soft worship music on and just rest in God's presence. Ask yourself how you're doing on this journey. You may want to get outdoors and breathe in some fresh air.

If you need some extra help to walk through this season, I recommend getting some professional help. Call a counselor. There is no shame in asking for help. We need it.

Reassure yourself: You are going to be okay. You are moving forward.

Write Out Your Own Prayer:

Day 11

For you have been made pure, set apart in the Anointed One, Jesus.
—1 Corinthians 1:2b

Set apart in Jesus means that you have royal access to the King of kings any time of the day or night. You are a child of the Most-High God.

What concerns you concerns God; what you need, He has.

The Holy Spirit is living inside of you. This is a very powerful truth. Think about it: The same Spirit that raised Christ from the dead lives within you (Romans 8:11).

The above doesn't mean that you won't have sadness or grief. It doesn't mean that you won't hurt. It doesn't mean that your world has not been turned upside down. This is part of the reality of being human.

God's Spirit living within you means that you have access to His love, His power, and His strength. All the promises in His eternal Word are yours. Grab hold of this truth as you are weaving in and out of wild emotions.

Christ in you is the hope of glory (Colossians 1:27). His presence in your heart makes all the difference. You have spiritual wisdom and understanding the world doesn't have. You are set apart in Him.

When you receive His strength and His love, you'll be able to handle all the emotions that strive for your attention His way. As you renew your mind with His Word, your attitudes change. You'll discover that when you read the Bible, you'll find comfort. You'll find answers on how the Lord is responding to you amidst your pain. God is extremely compassionate.

God is love, and His heart breaks for you.

PRAYER

Thank you, Lord, that you have set me apart in You. Thank you for making me pure. Thank you for cleansing my soul. God, I need Your comfort and Your presence today. I need to feel you near to me. I know You live within me, but I need to know what that looks like and what that feels like. Would You make Your presence real to me right now? Reveal the answers to the questions on my mind and in my heart. Let me hear Your voice of love. Bring healing to the deep places in my heart. Jesus'. Amen

QUIET PONDERINGS

Quiet yourself before the Lord. Put some soft worship music on and just rest in God's presence. Ask God to reveal where He has been throughout this journey. Ask Him to show You specific moments when He was displaying His love for you.

DAY 11

Write Out Your Own Prayer:

Day 12

> *Most sweet are his kisses, even his whispers of love. He is delightful in every way and perfect from every viewpoint.*
> —Song Of Songs 5:16a

Love can quench great turmoil.

Love can calm aggravation.

Love brings great peace.

When anger comes pounding on the door of our souls, demanding to take up residence, what we really need is love.

Have you ever wondered how God displays His love? He uniquely displays it to each of us. What brings you joy or comfort? I love sunsets. Just a glance at the beauty of the sunset does something on the inside of me. Sunsets are some of the most beautiful paintings. God is the painter, and the sky is His canvas. Next time you see a sunset that takes your breath away, pause for a moment. Receive His love through the magnificent colors of the sunset. It's like kisses from heaven.

Kisses from heaven often come in unexpected moments. Through a sunset, a song, or a comforting text from a friend. It's God reminding you that He sees you. It's like He's whispering, *I'm here with you. I know you're hurting. I know things feel like they are out of control, but I've got it. Nothing is too difficult for Me.*

Our God whispers His love to our hearts—even as we lie on the bed weeping with anger and anguish. We never know when our emotions will strike. One minute we are doing okay, and the next, we are punching pillows and yelling. God is with us. He holds our hearts with great compassion, and He will make His love known.

PRAYER

Thank you, Lord, that you have everything under control. Help me to believe that nothing is impossible or too difficult for You. I'm open to receiving Your love. Help me to see Your sweet kisses throughout the day. Jesus'. Amen.

QUIET PONDERINGS

Quiet yourself before the Lord. Put some soft worship music on and just rest in God's presence. Consider finding something beautiful that draws you close to the heart of God. It could be nature or a blank canvas and some paints. Anger can't stay long in the beauty of the Lord.

Take your time and allow His love to consume you. You are so loved.

DAY 12

Write Out Your Own Prayer:

STAGE 3

Bargaining & Regret

Day 13

Come to me, all you who are weary and burdened, and I will give you rest. Take my yoke upon you and learn from me, for I am gentle and humble in heart, and you will find rest for your souls. For my yoke is easy and my burden is light.
—Mathew 11:28-29 (NIV)

Have you ever felt overwhelmed by weariness? Have you ever felt the cares of life weighing you down? Have you ever longed for rest in your soul?

God longs to give you rest. He desires to take your unbearable load upon Himself. He longs to exchange your heavy burden for His easy yoke.

In the stage of bargaining and regret, your mind is like a racetrack. Is there anything you could have done differently to stop your loved one from taking his or her life? Did you say enough? Did you pray enough?

The burden can weigh on you so heavily at times.

In retrospect, did I do everything I could for either of my brothers? Yes, I did. At first, I wasn't sure. The questions were like bricks on my soul. The only way for me to lighten the load was to seek God. I continually read the Word and believed He would give me rest for my soul. On the especially hard days, I found myself running to God again and again.

Who could have ever known murder was in my brother's heart? I could never have imagined it. And I had no idea that he was someone who might take his own life. I just didn't see it. These realities were things I was forced to come to terms with.

Just so you know you're not alone, coming to terms with what happened is not an easy thing to do. Again, discovering a new normal after this kind of tragedy takes time. Be merciful with yourself. Some of your questions will have answers; some of them will not.

As you allow your friends to comfort you and God to bring you rest, your soul will find peace again.

Resist the urge to ignore the questions. Choose to face them. You will find the peace you long for as you seek God regarding your unanswerable questions. Until then, the questions without answers could easily be a source of torment.

Remember, God is ready and willing to give us rest. He simply asks us to come to Him with our weariness, with our burdens, and with our heavy hearts. He longs to teach us His ways so that we can find rest for our souls.

PRAYER

Thank you, Lord, that You receive me as I am. Thank you that I have no need to fear but that You will comfort me with Your love. Father, I have a lot of unanswered questions. Would You help me as I wrestle with them? Would You heal my broken heart and restore my soul? I know that You will. Help me to take You at Your Word. In Jesus' Name. Amen.

QUIET PONDERINGS

Quiet yourself before the Lord. Put some soft worship music on and just rest in God's presence. Do a divine exchange with God. For example, *"Father, here is my inadequacy. I feel like there was something more I could have said or done for my loved one. As I place this emotion in Your hands, what will You give me to replace it?"*

Write Out Your Own Prayer:

Day 14

You're my place of quiet retreat, and your wraparound presence becomes my shield as I wrap myself in your Word!
—Psalm 119:114

In the bargaining stage of grief, you may find yourself creating a lot of "what if" and "if only" statements. It's also not uncommon for religious individuals to try to make a deal or promise to God or a higher power in return for healing or relief from the grief and pain.[1]

Sometimes we want to push aside the facts regarding suicide. It's difficult to face reality, and it's painfully hard to admit the truth.

The bargaining stage of the grieving process was especially difficult for me after my first brother's death because he also took his ex-girlfriend's life. The guilt I felt for what my brother did was intense.

His ex-girlfriend had two young children; they will never see their mom again on earth. As I grieved, my mind kept replaying the possible scenarios of how the tragedy happened. I also imagined what her children's lives would be like without their mother.

---

1   https://www.healthline.com/health/stages-of-grief

I regretted not having done more for those children when I had the chance. Because I knew I would no longer have direct access to speak into their lives. That's the type of scenario when it's tempting to think, "If only I had invited them to church more, if only I had invited them over for dinner, if only I had said *this* instead of *that*." Then we want to bargain with God, pleading with Him to somehow turn back time and give us a do-over.

But of course, that's impossible. I didn't know what to do. So I decided to pray for them every day. I knew that prayer would impact them whether they knew someone was praying for them or not. This gave me a sense of comfort, knowing that I was doing something worthwhile. I didn't need to bargain with God and say, "God, I'll pray for them every day if you'll _____" (fill in the blank with the deal you're tempted to make).

Instead, I simply asked God to comfort my brother's ex-girlfriend's children. I prayed that God would make Himself known to them in tangible ways and to soften their hearts. I asked God to help them forgive so that they could walk in healing themselves. I prayed that the kids would someday come to know Jesus.

PRAYER

Father, help me to see situations and circumstances through Your eyes of truth. Cover me in Your wraparound presence and continue to make Yourself known to me. Bring order to my chaos, peace to my soul, and restore joy to my journey. I believe that nothing is impossible for You. Thank you for reminding me that I am not alone; You are with me. In Jesus' Name. Amen.

DAY 14

QUIET PONDERINGS

Quiet yourself before the Lord. Put some soft worship music on and just rest in God's presence. Take some time to simply breathe, then consider asking the Lord if there is someone He would like you to pray for today.

Write Out Your Own Prayer:

Day 15

The LORD your God is with you, the Mighty Warrior who saves.
He will take great delight in you.
—Zephaniah 3:17a (NIV)

Would you like some good news? God is with you. He is a mighty warrior, and He fights on your behalf. And despite your current emotional state, God takes great delight in you. He is not offended by your thoughts, emotions, or even your doubts. He simply loves you and takes delight in you.

Some days you'll want to skip the stages of grief. Some days, you'll wonder if this is your life, your reality. Did this tragedy truly happen to you, to your family? Unfortunately, if you're reading this book, then the answer is most likely yes.

It's easy to regret the days, the hours, the minutes before the incident. It's normal to wish you had done things differently, said something of significance, or even wish you had prayed harder.

One of the greatest gifts God gave humanity was free will, choice. This means every person is responsible for their own actions—whether those choices are wise or unwise.

It took me a long time to realize that my heart was heavy because I held myself responsible for what my brother did to his ex-girlfriend and her two children. The truth is…his actions were not my responsibility.

The only way to relieve this burden was to acknowledge it, then ask the Lord to forgive me. I blamed myself for my brother's actions, and it took a toll on my soul. I was unknowingly punishing myself by replaying the regrets in my head, over and over again.

Maybe you know what that feels like. Maybe you're blaming yourself for the choice of your loved one, living with borrowed regret. We don't have to take the punishment or pay the emotional debt. That's why Jesus went to the cross. He took the punishment and paid the debt already.

PRAYER

Jesus, thank you for paying the price for my sins, for the sins done to me, and the sins of others. Thank you that I do not have to live in consumed by regret for the actions of others. Open my eyes to see if I am holding myself responsible for things outside my control. Heal my heart and cleanse my soul. In Jesus' Name. Amen.

QUIET PONDERINGS

Quiet yourself before the Lord. Put some soft worship music on and just rest in God's presence. Ask the Lord if you have taken responsibility for the actions of your loved one. Write down whatever comes to mind, then ask the Lord what to do with what He shows you.

DAY 15

Write Out Your Own Prayer:

Day 16

We've been overwhelmed with grief; come now and overwhelm us with gladness. Replace our years of trouble with decades of delight.
—Psalm: 90:15

Shame.

It's strongly tied to this bargaining and regret stage of grief.

How is shame defined?

Brené Brown, author and researcher at the University of Houston, says this about shame:

> I define shame as the intensely painful feeling or experience of believing that we are flawed and therefore unworthy of love and belonging – something we've experienced, done, or failed to do makes us unworthy of connection.
>
> I don't believe shame is helpful or productive. In fact, I think shame is much more likely to be the source of destructive, hurtful behavior than the solution or cure.[2]

I believe that when shame and guilt travel together, trauma and tragedy are evident.

---

[2] https://brenebrown.com/blog/2013/01/14/shame-v-guilt

Sometimes shame is difficult to decipher because it likes to hide behind the mask of sorrow. Shame will tell us that we are bad, not that the actions or the choices we made were wrong.

Shame strives to define us negatively. For example, when I was around people, shame would tell me who I was. It would tell me I was defective and an embarrassment. It would whisper lies to my heart that there was no hope for me. I was unrepairable. Maybe you've heard these lies too.

In the days and weeks following the suicides, I received these lies as if they were truth instead of reaching out for connection with others, which I desperately needed. I tried to isolate myself. I wanted to avoid people because I was ashamed of what my brothers had done.

Friend, resist the urge to isolate. It's okay to spend some time alone. Nevertheless, try to stay connected to at least two or three people. You don't have to be open to everyone, but it's important to allow a few select and safe people to walk with you through these difficult times.

PRAYER

Father, thank you that those who look to You are never covered in shame. Father, it's hard to imagine that You can replace my sorrow and grief with joy and gladness, but I want to believe. I want my heart to laugh again, to hope again, and to believe again. Today, I'm asking You to reveal where shame has held my heart prisoner with its lies. Show me the truth and set me free. In Jesus' Name. Amen.

QUIET PONDERINGS

Quiet yourself before the Lord. Put some soft worship music on and just rest in God's presence. Take a few moments and write out a list of people or things that bring you joy or make you laugh. Then, choose something on your list and do it. Be intentional today to do something or watch something that will make you laugh. Laughter is good medicine for the soul.

Write Out Your Own Prayer:

Day 17

My darling bride, my private paradise, fastened to my heart.
—Song Of Songs 4:12

How are you feeling today? Are you feeling today? Or, are you feeling numb, wondering if it's possible ever to feel positive emotions again?

I get it. I understand going through the motions. I know what it's like to get up every morning and try to make it through the day so you can go back to bed.

Every day you think of a new "What if…" question.

Would my loved one have answered? Would the outcome be different?

It's so tempting to ask these types of questions repeatedly. The truth is…these questions are often unproductive because we will never know the answer. These questions only lead us to more questions, not solutions. This only leads to frustration.

> Frustration is defined as *"a feeling of dissatisfaction, often accompanied by anxiety or depression, resulting from unfulfilled needs or unresolved problems."*[3]

---

[3] https://www.dictionary.com/browse/frustration

You are not alone in your feeling of frustration. We often get frustrated because we can't control a situation; we have no authority or ability to bring about the desired result.

Therefore, it is so important to stay close to the Lord. He said that He has fastened us to His heart. We are permanently linked to His heart. Think about it. Another word for fastened is secure; we are securely fastened to the Lord.

Don't be afraid to share your genuine thoughts with God. He longs for us to share our frustrations, our questions with Him. While He is already aware of what we are thinking and what we are feeling, when we talk about them with Him, it opens the door for Him to comfort and heal our hearts.

PRAYER

Father, Your Word says that You have fastened me to Your heart. God, it's difficult for me to imagine that right now. My mind is flooded with questions that don't have answers. Honestly, I'm frustrated, and a part of me may still be angry that my life is now defined by having a loved one that took their own life. I don't want to be frustrated. I don't want to be angry. I just want to feel like I can breathe again. Since I'm fastened to Your heart, will You help me? I'm not even sure what I need at this moment, but I do know You can provide it. Help me to feel Your presence—even now. In Jesus' Name. Amen.

QUIET PONDERINGS

Quiet yourself before the Lord. Put some soft worship music on and just rest in God's presence. Take a few moments and ask God what it practically looks like or feels like to be fastened to His heart. Ask Him how to live this reality out every day.

DAY 17

Write Out Your Own Prayer:

Day 18

In my distress I cried out to you, the delivering God, and from your temple-throne you heard my troubled cry, and my sobs went right into your heart.
—Psalm 18:16

God is full of mercy and compassion. Our God is not only defined by love; He IS love.

When our hearts are heavy, we can cry out to Him. When our tears outnumber our words, He is with us. Our sobs go straight into His heart.

When I was walking through the loss of my late husband, I would read the Bible and talk with the Lord. But there were still moments when my pain would seemingly overtake His truth. It wasn't always easy to hear God; some days, it felt like it took more effort than I had to give.

But that's where this verse comes in. We can cry out to Him with confidence that our pain is piercing His heart.

"*[God] reached down from on high and took hold of me; he drew me out of deep waters.*"[4] He comes to us. He reaches out with His mighty hands, and He takes out of us the calamity and chaos. He draws us to himself. God knows and understands our pain.

---

4   Psalm 18:16 NIV

I remember when I had to go to the funeral home to order my late husband's headstone. I couldn't do it. I didn't want to do it. I dodged calls from the funeral home and my family members. Why? Because in my heart, ordering the headstone meant everything was final.

In my head, I had convinced myself that if I don't order the headstone, then everything will be okay. I just want everything to be okay again. I just want to get to a place of normal. Life is not normal without my husband. Therefore, if I don't order the headstone, then I don't have to face the truth that he's really gone.

It's a painful but important step when our hearts finally understand that our loved one is never coming back.

It's okay to cry. It's okay to let out wails from deep within your soul that words cannot express. Crying doesn't make you weak; crying proves your strength because you're willing to admit that you're experiencing some of life's most painful emotions yet choosing to move forward anyway.

So, let it out. Your sobs pierce God's heart.

PRAYER

Father, awaken my soul to Your presence right now. Help me to release the pain that I've stuffed deep down inside. Please help me to let it out, to let it go. Show me in tangible ways how my pain pierces Your heart. I need a manifestation of Your love in my life today. Reveal Your love toward me in a way that I can understand. I ask this in Jesus' name. Amen.

QUIET PONDERINGS

Quiet yourself before the Lord. Put some soft worship music on and just rest in God's presence. You may even want to turn the music off and simply sit in silence today. Close your eyes and imagine Heavenly Father, Jesus, or Holy Spirit holding you as you cry.

DAY 18

Write Out Your Own Prayer:

STAGE 4

Depression

Day 19

All who are oppressed may come to Yahweh as a high shelter in the time of trouble, a perfect hiding place.
—Psalm 9:9

Our God is a shelter in time of trouble.

How many times will God shelter us? Once? Twice? God is our continual shelter. There is no check-out time. We can always hide in Him.

What does it look like to hide in God?

It looks like being in the safest place you can imagine. It looks like being in a place without fear. It looks like being in a place where you not only feel safe but also protected. That's what it looks like to hide in God. It's the place where the world and the enemy can't find you or harm you because you are so secure in His loving presence.

However, some days it's difficult to feel, let alone feel safe. The next stage of grief is depression.

> "Depression is a mood disorder that involves a persistent feeling of sadness and loss of interest. It is different from the mood fluctuations that people regularly experience as a part of life."[5]

[5] https://www.medicalnewstoday.com/articles/8933#definition

It is normal to feel depressed for a while following the death of a loved one. However, if you find that your depression lasts for an extended amount of time, please contact a health professional for some assistance.

Visiting a counselor or taking medication as prescribed does not mean that you have failed or do not trust God. There are times in life when the assistance of others helps to accelerate our healing. There is no shame and no condemnation if a counselor or medication is needed to help you. You can trust God for your healing and hide in Him while obtaining professional assistance.

PRAYER

Father, thank you that You made a way for us to run into Your fortress. Help me to feel Your constant protection daily. Show me Your love in tangible ways. Manifest Your presence and awaken my soul to Your promised restoration. Send an angel to give me a heavenly shot of joy. You said that Your joy is my strength, my protection. I could really use some of Your joy today. In Jesus' name. Amen.

QUIET PONDERINGS

Quiet yourself before the Lord. Put some soft worship music on and just rest in God's presence. Ask the Lord to send an angel to minister to you. Take a few moments and write down how you're feeling or if you see or hear anything from the Lord.

DAY 19

Write Out Your Own Prayer:

Day 20

In all of my affliction I find great comfort in your promises, for they have kept me alive!
—Psalm 119:50

God is good.

Is that hard for you to believe right now?

God is good—all the time. It may come across as a trite Christian saying, but if you are willing to believe it, you'll begin to look at the world through a different lens.

You'll be able to say as David did in Psalm 27:

> Yet I believe with all my heart that I will see again your goodness, Yahweh, in the land of life eternal. Here's what I've learned through it all: *Don't give up*; don't be impatient; be entwined as one with the Lord. Be brave and courageous, and never lose hope. Yes, keep on waiting—*for he will never disappoint you.*[6]

God will not disappoint you because He is the complete embodiment of love and goodness. The devil will lie to you. Friends and family will fail to meet your expectations, but God will continually comfort you.

---

[6] Psalm 27:13-14

Sometimes our friends say the wrong thing. They say something that is the exact opposite of what we need to hear. Resist the temptation to let their words throw you into a depression because you believe no one understands and no one ever will. Believe that their motive was pure—especially if they have never experienced a loved one taking his or her own life.

I remember that there were many days that I just sat in my living room all day feeling sad. I didn't know how to handle things. I knew I couldn't do this every day. It wouldn't be healthy.

At that time, a friend came over and advised, "You need to do something, Susan."

I believe that my friend wanted to help me, but what I really needed was someone to listen to me, not try a "quick fix" on me.

There is no quick fix. There is no "snapping out of it." You're bleeding on the inside and need time to heal. As you know, healing is a process. God is with you every step of the way. He is patient.

I would encourage you to find two or three promises in the Bible that speak to your heart. Read them out loud. Memorize them. Believe in God's goodness and come into agreement with His promises for you.

Choose to worship God and confess that He is good, especially when it doesn't *feel* that way. Declare that you will see the goodness of the Lord in the land of the living. Then keep declaring it until your feelings finally catch up with your declaration.

Remember to be patient with yourself. Choose to be merciful to yourself. And whatever you do, don't give up. Keep moving forward one step at a time.

PRAYER

Father, I choose as an act of my will to believe that You are good. Your Word says that You inhabit the praises of Your people. Your Word says that You are close to the brokenhearted. It says that a bruised reed You will not break. My heart is hurting, and my entire life feels bruised. I need Your presence. I need Your love. I need Your healing. Help me to walk this path that I didn't choose for myself or my family. You didn't choose it for us either. Help me to see Your goodness today. Help me to see and experience Your goodness in my life in this land called living. In Jesus' name. Amen.

QUIET PONDERINGS

Quiet yourself before the Lord. Put some soft worship music on and just rest in God's presence. Take a few moments and ask God to reveal the ways that He has been good to you. Write down what comes to your mind. If you struggle, start out by writing the attributes or characteristics of God that bring you comfort. As you do this, I believe that a sense of peace and joy will minister to your soul, as the dark clouds of depression begin to slowly blow away.

Write Out Your Own Prayer:

Day 21

> I will worship and praise your name, O Lord, for it is precious to me. Through you I'm saved—rescued from every trouble.
> —Psalm 54:6b-7a

I'm going to let you in on a secret. You can have joy and sorrow at the same time.

Too often, we believe that everything is *either/or* in life. You either have joy, or you have sorrow. But what if, for a season, you experienced both?

I want to permit you to feel happy and joyful while still experiencing the pain of loss in your soul. You are not betraying your loved one by living life. In fact, your willingness to experience moments of joy is an act of worship.

When I was walking through this valley of death and destruction, I didn't know a lot about God. I was learning about Him and His words. I was learning that He was worthy of my trust.

But what I wanted was to live without pain. I wanted to pray one moment, and in the next moment, I desired for the pain in my heart to be gone. Frankly, that didn't happen.

Instead, God walked beside me in my pain. He taught me to run to Him and allow Him to strengthen me. He encouraged me to worship Him by focusing on His goodness. He comforted me as I understood that He is enough. And, as I learned that He was enough, He showed me that I was enough too.

You may need to tell yourself and your circumstances that God is enough. Remind yourself that God is stronger than the pain, bigger than the mistakes, and more worthy than any fear.

As you meditate on God's greatness, you'll discover that His presence will fill your heart and mind. His peace will overtake you. You'll be able to rest in His love. God will quiet you with His love and help you sleep through the night.

PRAYER

Father, I exalt Your name. I give You all the glory and honor. Thank you for rescuing me from all trouble. Thank You for helping me to choose joy even in the midst of sorrow. Thank you for singing songs of deliverance over me. Open my ears to hear the songs of Heaven today. Put a new song in my heart—a song of praise to You. I believe that You are good. Shine Your light in the midst of my darkness. Lead me out of this valley of death and destruction and onto the paths of righteousness for Your name's sake. Lead me to green pastures and still waters. Restore my soul. In Jesus' name. Amen.

QUIET PONDERINGS

Quiet yourself before the Lord. You may want to put some soft worship music on and just rest in God's presence. Take a few moments and sing a song to the Lord. It doesn't have to be long. It doesn't have to be pretty. If nothing comes to mind at first, sing "Jesus Loves Me." Today, choose joy.

DAY 21

Write Out Your Own Prayer:

Day 22

You've kept track of all my wandering and my weeping. You've stored my many tears in your bottle—not one will be lost.
—Psalm 56:8

God keeps track of all our wandering and our weeping—and doesn't judge us for it.

The Father is showing us His gentle compassion and love.

God cares so much about our pain and suffering that He saves every tear. Each tear that releases from our eyes He catches in a bottle. Every drop is precious to Him. He weeps with us and feels what we feel.

One of the many reasons we can feel depressed is because we tell ourselves, *"People are tired of my tears and sadness. I need to put on a happy face and pretend."* You may even have well-meaning people imply that it's time to move on from grieving.

When the world tells you the time for tears is over, that's exactly the moment you can turn to God.

You can cry on His shoulder whenever you need to, for as long as you need to. He will never brush off your tears. He will never pressure you to "pull yourself together" for someone else's sake. Instead, He stores every one of your tears in a bottle. What a beautiful picture. Every tear you cry matters to Him.

Have you ever wondered how big that bottle of tears is? The beautiful thing is that tears are a language that God understands. Our tears are prayers that our words cannot form.

Circumstances will change. In time, things will get easier. But you can't rush the process just to please or appease someone else. For now, trust that God will heal all the hurting hearts. Believe that He will somehow take what the enemy meant for harm and bring forth something good from it.

PRAYER

Father, thank you for watching over me in my wanderings. Thank you for catching all my tears in a bottle. Thank you for caring about me. Thank you for renewing my hope. Thank you for Your kindness and compassion toward me. It's such a precious and intimate thing to catch and hold my tears in a bottle. Thank you for giving me this picture of Your tenderness toward me. In Jesus' name. Amen.

QUIET PONDERINGS

Quiet yourself before the Lord. You may want to put some soft worship music on and just rest in God's presence. You may want to ask God to show you the bottle that holds your tears. What shape is it? What does it look like? You may want to sketch it out as a reminder.

DAY 22

Write Out Your Own Prayer:

Day 23

The comfort of your love takes away my fear. I'll never be lonely, for you are near. You become my delicious feast even when my enemies dare to fight. You anoint me with the fragrance of your Holy Spirit; you give me all I can drink of you until my cup overflows.
—Psalm 23:4b-5

The comfort of God's love takes away our fear. Even though our loved one has passed on, we don't have to be lonely. God is with us.

As we learn to allow God to be our feast, to be the thing that brings us soul satisfaction, we will not fear even when the enemy dares to fight.

We can sit at the table with Jesus as the disciples did. We can take the elements of communion. He said that His body was broken for us. He said that His blood was poured out for us. His sacrifice renewed God's eternal covenant with humanity. It gives us the right to drink of His healing, hope, love, peace, and safety.

We feast on His goodness, and it gives us the strength to keep going. His presence in our lives helps us maintain our sanity despite our sorrow.

God will anoint us with the fragrance of His Spirit. God is generous. He gives us more than enough. God doesn't just fill our cup once, but He continually fills our cup so much that it overflows.

It's probably hard to imagine life's cup overflowing with goodness right now. But there will be a day when you're able to dry your tears. You'll discover that new normal—the one you didn't ask for, but will adjust to in time. You'll experience God's goodness in the land of the living.

That doesn't mean that you won't miss your loved one. Of course, you will. You'll still wonder where he or she would be, what he would be doing, would she have had children, etc. But if you'll sit at the table with Jesus when you ask these questions, He will help you process through them.

PRAYER

Father, thank you that I can sit at Your table and eat of Your goodness. Thank you for providing me with a safe place when the enemy dares to fight. Thank you that You have promised me victory, and you are helping me overcome the attacks of my adversaries. Teach me, Lord. Teach me as I sit at Your table. Teach me how to receive Your goodness. Teach me how to drink and have my cup overflow. Cleanse my heart today and renew Your covenant with me. In Jesus' name. Amen.

QUIET PONDERINGS

Quiet yourself before the Lord. You may want to put some soft worship music on and just rest in God's presence. What do you need from the Lord? Ask Him for it and believe that you have received it.

DAY 23

Write Out Your Own Prayer:

Day 24

So why would I fear the future? Only goodness and tender love pursue me all the days of my life.
—Psalm 23:6a

As I was writing this devotional, my oldest sister graduated from this earth to her true home in heaven. She battled cancer for more than two years.

My sister was one of my best friends. Our kids spent summers together. We consistently traveled to see each other. We never let more than three or four months go by without visiting. I love her, and I miss her tremendously.

Maybe you understand this sorrow: the pain of losing not only a loved one who took his or her own life but also experiencing the pain of those who have passed on for other reasons.

Fear wants you to fall into its trap. Fear wants you to begin to wonder, who's next? Fear wants you to believe that God didn't hear or answer your prayers.

Jesus came to bring us life, not death. In fact, He suffered and died to save us from death.

Fear can paralyze and hold us captive in an unhealthy place in our soul and spirit.

Love never brings fear, for fear is always related to punishment. But love's perfection drives the fear *of punishment far* from our hearts. Whoever walks constantly afraid of *punishment* has not reached love's perfection.[7]

Fear wants us to believe that everything that happens to us stems from something we did or didn't do. Friend, it's not true. There are consequences to our choices. I do not deny that. But we need to be well-balanced. It is important to remember that we live in a fallen world. God does not put sickness on us to teach us a lesson or to punish us. These things are just part of the painful reality of life on earth.

But there are good things in this life, too. The Bible says every good and perfect gift is from above. If it's not good, it's not God. And even though it's hard some days, we can remind ourselves that life on earth also includes much beauty, goodness and love. Whatever happened today or in the past, we can have hope for a brighter future because God is working all things together for our good.

PRAYER

Father, thank you for loving me. Thank you for meeting me right where I'm at emotionally and mentally. Your Word says that I don't need to fear the future. God, I admit I have some fears in my heart. I need Your love to rescue me. I need Your love to expel the fear due to questions without answers. I open my heart to receive Your love. Fill me with Your presence and consume me with Your love. In Jesus' name. Amen.

QUIET PONDERINGS

Quiet yourself before the Lord. You may want to find an audio version of your favorite Psalm. Just listen to it and allow your spirit and soul to receive its truth.

---

7   1 John 4:18

DAY 24

Dare to make plans for the future. It's hard when so many thoughts from the past are overwhelming you. But that's exactly why you need to do it. Pull out your calendar and set a future date when you and those you love most will go do something fun. Yes, something fun. It doesn't have to be next week. Maybe you think you'll be ready six months from now. Or this time next year. It's entirely up to you. But it is time to plan again.

Write Out Your Own Prayer:

STAGE 5

Acceptance

Day 25

*Surely He has borne our griefs
And carried our sorrows.*
—Isaiah 53:4a (NKJV)

God understands your grief. He has carried your sorrows. He's aware that life for you will never be the same. What used to be normal for you is different now.

In the wake of my family members' deaths, people around me continued with life as normal. Questions about everyday activities for the kids used to anger me because no one knew how I felt inside. Life was making me move forward, and I wasn't ready.

> Acceptance is not necessarily a happy or uplifting stage of grief. It doesn't mean you've moved past the grief or loss. It does, however, mean that you've accepted it and have come to understand what it means in your life now.[8]

You have a new reality. You don't have to like it, but you do have to learn to live with it.

I know it's hard. I know it's not what you want to do. I know you'd rather rewind the clock and revert to a time when everything was happy and normal. You're not alone.

---

8   https://www.healthline.com/health/stages-of-grief#acceptance

As you navigate to discover a new rhythm to life, God is with you. He's not going anywhere. Sunshine or rain, God will never leave you or forsake you.

You may find it helpful to do something that your loved one enjoyed. For example, my younger brother loved flower gardens and trees. To help me move forward, I planted a tree in his honor.

PRAYER

Father, thank you that Jesus bore my grief and carried my sorrows. Thank you that You know what it's like to lose a loved one. Jesus, thank you for choosing to come to earth, for choosing to suffer, and for choosing to save me from my sin. Help me today to remember the things I love about my loved one. Help me to remember what was important to him or her. Give me an idea of how I can keep their memory alive in my heart as I discover a new normal for me. In Jesus' name. Amen.

QUIET PONDERINGS

Quiet yourself before the Lord. You may want to put some soft worship music on and just rest in God's presence.

Ask God what you can do in remembrance of your loved one. What did they love to do? God will give you a way to keep their memory and presence alive in your heart. Take some time and write out your favorite memory with him or her.

DAY 25

Write Out Your Own Prayer:

Day 26

And I find that the strength of Christ's explosive power infuses me to conquer every difficulty.
—Philippians 4:13

Everyone probably has their own definition of what acceptance means.

For me, I've accepted the fact that my brothers didn't think of how their choices would affect our families or me. I accept that the pain they were living in was more than they could handle themselves.

Acceptance also means that I've decided to make peace with their decision and put one foot in front of the other. I've accepted that there will be questions that have no answers.

Be encouraged. If you're wondering if you will ever get through this dark season in your life, you will. Nevertheless, it doesn't just happen overnight. No one's journey is the same. Every individual has a different process of overcoming this difficult time.

Know this: The revelation of Jesus Christ and his explosive power gives you the strength to conquer every difficulty. You are already an overcomer. You are already more than a conqueror.

God is with you. God is for you.

Just remember to be patient with yourself and others. Keep moving forward and stay close to Jesus. Remove the expectation that your healing process has to unfold according to someone else's timetable. God has all the time in the world. When you are ready to embrace the final step of acceptance, God will be ready to help you.

PRAYER

Father, thank you for Your patience and long-suffering with me. I could not do this without You. You know what long-suffering is, and Your heart is so tender to me. I need you. I need Your strength to infuse me with Your power. Continue to give me a revelation of who You are and how close You are to me. In Jesus' name. Amen.

QUIET PONDERINGS

Quiet yourself before the Lord. You may want to put some soft worship music on and just rest in God's presence.

You may find it fun to gather favorite items of clothing from your loved one and make a blanket or stuffed animal. If you're not into sewing, you could find a seamstress to do it for you. It's a wonderful way to remember them.

DAY 26

Write Out Your Own Prayer:

Day 27

The one who calls you by name is trustworthy and will thoroughly complete his work in you.
—1 Thessalonians 5:24

Let the Word of God become the foundation for your life.

There was a time when I believed what was happening to me was bigger than my God. I was so wrong. God is the source of all LIFE. God is the source of all GOODNESS. God is the source of all POWER.

God taught me His ways. I learned and came to accept that He is reliable, trustworthy, and faithful.

When someone proves themselves to you, it changes what you believe. It changes how you live. It changes the lens you look through. Your heart starts pumping again with new hope and new life. You start breathing again. You surge upward and forward from the bottom of an ocean where you've been holding your breath for so long. Your lungs have been so tired and weary.

"The one who calls you by name is trustworthy and will thoroughly complete his work in you."[9] God's name is

---

9   1 Thessalonians 5:24

Trustworthy. He is faithful; He will continue to complete the work He started in you.

We overcome these horrific life-changing events in our lives by creating our foundation from God's Word. We stand and move forward on the truth of His eternal Word.

God is building your confidence and trust in Him. You matter so much to Him! He wants to demonstrate His character and impart a deeper knowledge of who He is to you.

PRAYER

Father, thank you for being trustworthy. Thank you for your faithfulness. Help me to trust You with all my heart. You said that if I trusted You and leaned not on my own understanding but acknowledged You in all that I am doing, You would put me on a straight path. I want to trust You with my entire being. Continue to show me that You are faithful and true. In Jesus' name. Amen.

QUIET PONDERINGS

Quiet yourself before the Lord. You may want to put some soft worship music on and just rest in God's presence. You may want to thank God for His faithfulness. Ask Him to tell you about the work He is doing in you. How can you partner with Him at this time?

DAY 27

Write Out Your Own Prayer:

Day 28

Now faith is confidence in what we hope for and assurance about what we do not see.
—Hebrew 11:1 (NIV)

Martin Luther King, Jr. once said, "Take the first step in faith. You don't have to see the whole staircase, just take the first step."[10]

As we move into this place of acceptance, our view may be somewhat obstructed by various emotions and other people's voices.

Acceptance can be likened to navigating a vehicle in a downpour at night. It's foggy, rainy, and the road is winding. If your lights are on and you drive slowly, the trip will be safer. Sometimes, you have to pull over and pause to allow the storm to pass. But eventually, you make it to your destination.

You are going to make it. You are going to be okay.

As you travel on this road of acceptance, there may be twists and turns in the road. But know that you are on the journey, and God is with you. There's no speed limit minimum or maximum. You can travel at your own pace. Choosing every

---

10 https://www.goodreads.com/quotes/199214-take-the-first-step-in-faith-you-don-t-have-to

day to put your car in drive and move forward is faith in action.

I'm so proud of you. More importantly, God is proud of you.

If life gets overwhelming, pull off to the side and breathe for a bit. You've already come so far. Keep going.

You are doing so well. Remember, it's okay to be patient with yourself.

PRAYER

Father, I have decided to move forward in faith with You. I accept what I cannot change. Thank you for meeting me every step of the way. I need you. Warn me if I need to pull over and be revived again. You are my strength. Thank you for all You have done and are doing in me. In Jesus' Name. Amen.

QUIET PONDERINGS

Quiet yourself before the Lord. You may want to put some soft worship music on and just rest in God's presence. Take some time to reflect on your journey. Acknowledge how far you've come.

DAY 28

Write Out Your Own Prayer:

Day 29

Open my eyes to see the miracle-wonders
hidden in Scripture.
—Psalm 119:18

One morning as I was walking and enjoying the beauty of God's creation. I saw some beautiful, lush greenery. Right in the middle, standing tall above the rest of the plants, was a pure white iris. It was captivating. I realized I was ready to look for and appreciate beauty again. I was accepting, finally, that not everything was dark – there was beauty if I was willing to open my eyes and see it.

Are you ready to appreciate beauty again? Are you ready to open your eyes to the good that's around you? Even if you don't feel ready at this moment, why not make this your prayer: "Lord, open my eyes to see. Open my eyes to see beauty, and happiness and new opportunities."

The iris was a beautiful white. It made me think of purity and holiness. God sees you as pure and holy.

Did you know that irises are hardy flowers? They can grow almost anywhere as long as they have water and sunshine.

If you stay connected to the Light (Jesus) and stay planted in the soil of His word, you will be able to thrive regardless of circumstances. Whether you are planted in a garden or in the wild, you will be able to grow.

Just like the iris amid the greenery, as you allow God's love for you to transform you, you will stand out from this world. People are watching to see if Jesus will help you overcome this tragedy.

When you've discovered your new normal, the key is to continue looking for the miracle-wonders hidden in God's Word. Don't stop pursuing His presence. Don't stop seeking His comfort. Don't stop receiving His love.

You've made so much progress. Ask God to open your eyes to miracle wonders right in front of you. He will.

PRAYER

Father, thank you for being You. Thank you for encouraging my soul. Thank you that You see me as a pure and holy vessel, fit for use in Your kingdom. Lord, I believe that You are the gardener. Plant me where You need me. Help me to see how far You have brought me. Show me what You have pruned from me so that I can become fruitful. Thank you for healing my heart and bringing hope to my soul. You are so good to me. In Jesus' name. Amen.

QUIET PONDERINGS

Quiet yourself before the Lord. You may want to put some soft worship music on and just rest in God's presence. Ask Him to show you more miracle wonders in His word.

In honor of your loved one, you may want to make their favorite meal and invite family and friends to share memories.

DAY 29

Write Out Your Own Prayer:

Day 30

Yahweh, lead me in the pathways of your pleasure just like you promised me you would, or else my enemies will conquer me. Smooth out your road in front of me, straight and level, so that I will know where to walk.
—Psalm 5:8a (TPT)

You have been incredibly courageous to walk this road. You didn't choose it. You wouldn't have chosen it. Nevertheless, you have been so brave to face your emotions and choose to trust in God.

> Merriam-Webster defines courage as: "Mental or moral strength to venture, persevere, and withstand danger, fear, or difficulty."[11]

> Another definition of courage says it is the "strength of mind to carry on in spite of danger."[12]

Courage permits us to face extreme difficulties and to do it without fear.

This is possible because our Heavenly Father helps us face our fears and overcome them. The truth is that everyone experiences fear. It's what we choose to do with it that determines our outcome.

---

11   https://www.merriam-webster.com/dictionary/courage
12   https://www.merriam-webster.com/thesaurus/courage

Pushing through fear is less frightening than living with the bigger underlying fear that comes from a feeling of helplessness. This is the one truth that some people have difficulty understanding. When you push through the fear, you will feel such a sense of relief as your feeling of helplessness subsides. You will wonder why you did not take action sooner. You will become more and more aware that you can truly handle anything that life hands you.[13]
—Susan Jeffers, Ph.D.

The Psalmist understood this too, as he cried out to God, "Smooth out your road in front of me, straight and level, so that I will know where to walk."[14] God does this as we take steps of faith to overcome our fears.

We are victorious in God. As you continue to move forward, you will experience the pleasure of His pathways. You will see His promises become your reality as you continue to walk with Him and stay close to His heart.

God is for you, and you are gaining victorious ground with each step.

PRAYER

Father, thank you that Your love expels fear. Thank you for helping me to be strong and courageous even when I felt weak. Thank you that my enemies will not overtake me. Thank you for smoothing out the road in front of me. Thank you for making my path clear. You are my ever-present help. You are the solid rock on which I stand. You are the source of my strength, courage, and hope. You are the reason that I have the ability to move forward in this life. Thank you for all that You have done for me. In Jesus' name. Amen.

---

13   http://www.susanjeffers.com/home/5truths.cfm
14   Psalm 5:8

DAY 30

QUIET PONDERINGS

Quiet yourself before the Lord. You may want to put some soft worship music on and just rest in God's presence. Ask God to show you how He has smoothed out the road before you.

GRIEVING SUICIDE

Write Out Your Own Prayer:

Conclusion

Throughout the writing of this book, it has become apparent that Jesus held me, guided me, and kept me when I was without the strength to carry on. There was a time when I didn't believe I would ever get out of the dark night of the soul. But thanks be to God, I am healthy and whole. I love life again. That's what I call a miracle.

God's Word is ALIVE, and He is FAITHFUL. I owed a debt I couldn't pay. So, I've chosen to give God my life and become a living sacrifice full of GRATITUDE AND PRAISE to Him.

My prayer for you is that as you read the pages within this devotional, your heart started to beat again. It was my earnest desire that God would massage your heart back to life.

My heart is that you understood the stages of grief so that you would not fear them. I trust that you now know that what you are feeling and experiencing is normal, given the tragedy in your life.

You are greatly loved. God is for you and will never leave your side. He longs to be your healer and comforter.

With His help, you will make it to the other side of this valley. And when you do, my prayer is that you will help someone else see that Jesus wants to be their healer, too.

Forever grateful to my Lord.

—Susan

I Pray You Were Blessed

I pray this devotional has helped you move forward in your healing journey. I would be so grateful if you could share your testimony of how this book touched your heart. You can do so on Amazon by visiting: review.SusanStotts.com

Your story might just be the one that encourages another person to take the first step to healing after loss and grief.

Your Sister in Christ,

Susan Stotts

Acknowledgments

I want to thank my Lord and Savior for showing me what faithfulness and pure love looks like.

Brian Stotts, my husband, relentlessly cheered me on and filled up the slack with everything else. Thank You!

Dustin Cichosz – who is so talented and committed to seeing this book get into the hands of everyone who needs it. Thank you for coming over at the spur of the moment when I would lose something on the computer and helping me find it again.

To all of my friends and family: I cannot name them all for fear I'd leave someone out. Thank you! I could not have done this without your prayers, encouragement, and faithfulness to this process so that healing will come to many.

Thank you, Kristin Reeg, for your gift of capturing the words of my heart and bringing life and light to them.

LAST BUT NOT LEAST, Donna Partow, what an exemplary guide you have been. You have stretched me; you have pulled out of me things I didn't even know existed within me. Your tireless hard work and detailed attention to every part of this book were so exceptional. Know that I value you and appreciate all that you have done for me. Thank you for the encouragement and believing in me that God will use this for his Glory.

About the Author

Susan Stotts is an inspirational Christian speaker who shares her compelling life story of triumph over the tragedy of multiple suicides in her family. Her passion is to see families brought to healing and restoration after loss.

She has traveled and shared her testimony of triumph over tragedy throughout the United States and Canada.

Susan and her husband, Brian, live in Northern California where they run a small business than has been in their family for more than 50 years. They have eight children, 12 grandchildren, and one great-granddaughter.

You can learn more about her speaking ministry at www.SusanStotts.com

Made in the USA
Monee, IL
04 December 2021